IN LINE

to the

THRONE

IN LINE
to the
THRONE

Prince Charles and the other 29 in waiting

Tobias Anthony & Jeremy Cassar with illustrations by Oslo Davis

Smith
Street
Books

Contents

Introduction 6

The Royal Family Tree 8

In Line to the Throne

#1   Prince Charles 10

#2   Prince William 14

#3   Prince George 18

#4   Princess Charlotte 22

#5   Prince Henry 26

#6   Prince Andrew 30

#7   Princess Beatrice 34

#8   Princess Eugenie 38

#9   Prince Edward 42

#10 James, Viscount Severn 46

#11 Lady Louise Windsor 50

#12 Princess Anne 52

#13 Peter Phillips 54

#14 Savannah Phillips 56

#15 Isla Phillips 58

#16 Zara Phillips 60

#17 Mia Grace Tindall 62

#18 David Amstrong-Jones, Viscount Linley 64

#19 Charles Amstrong-Jones 66

#20 Margarita Amstrong-Jones 68

#21 Lady Sarah Chatto 70

#22 Samuel Chatto 71

#23 Arthur Chatto 72

#24 Prince Richard 73

#25 Major Alexander Windsor 74

#26 Xan Windsor, Lord Culloden 75

#27 Lady Cosima Windsor 76

#28 Lady Davina Lewis 77

#29 Senna Lewis 78

#30 Tāne Lewis 79

Introduction

I t probably won't be much of a surprise to anybody if, after Queen Elizabeth II is finished queening about for the better part of the last century, her grandson, Prince William, Duke of Cambridge, will rightfully take the throne as King William V. Of course, this logical scenario would be loved by all except poor old Prince Charles, who has been waiting for his mother to shuffle off this mortal coil since 1952. Sadly, the chance of Charlie passing over his opportunity to be king in favour of his son is, perhaps understandably, remote.

However, the son of Prince Charles and Lady Diana has seemed destined for the role ever since he first started losing his hair, sometime during the early stages of puberty. And why shouldn't he ascend to the top of the royal pile? It's what the people want, after all. Well, that, and to know what exactly Kate will be wearing at the coronation.

But the future is not set, and anything could happen between now and the day Liz decides to hang up her sceptre and call it quits for good. With Will helicoptering himself all over England and playing ridiculous amounts of charity polo matches, there's always the chance that the young prince may find himself losing his saintly head to a rotor blade or copping a stray mallet to the temple, and if that were the case then we feel pretty confident that, at this stage, neither George nor

Charlotte are exactly fit for Royal duties. So, when you think of it like that, the throne is pretty much up for grabs.

In Line to the Throne provides a breakdown of Charles, Will and the other 28 runners-up to the throne. We're willing to assume you didn't know there could be a King Xan or a King Tāne one day. And you probably didn't realise there's a Queen Cosima in the running as well.

We've compiled a mix of historical non-fiction, biography and real facts for your reading pleasure. Plus we've thrown in a few fibs for good measure as well (we can't give them the royal treatment all year round). Whether you're a staunch monarchist or more of a republican-leaning type, it doesn't hurt to acquaint yourself with Britain's top Royals — they could be in charge one day, after all.

So go ahead and have a browse, here are the thirty Royals in line to the throne.

The Royal Family Tree
Line of succession

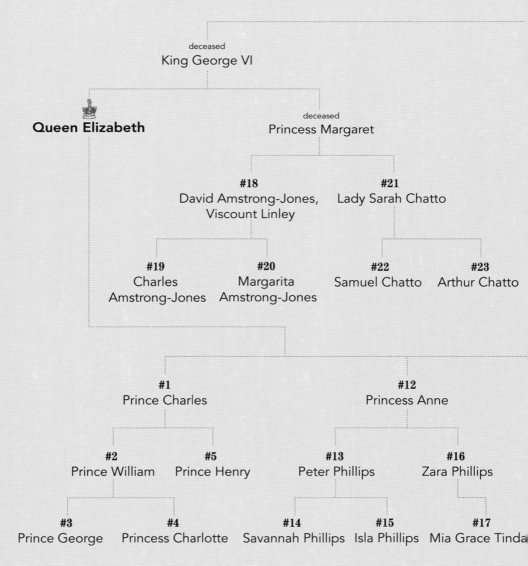

deceased
King George VI

Queen Elizabeth

deceased
Princess Margaret

#18
David Amstrong-Jones,
Viscount Linley

#21
Lady Sarah Chatto

#19
Charles
Amstrong-Jones

#20
Margarita
Amstrong-Jones

#22
Samuel Chatto

#23
Arthur Chatto

#1
Prince Charles

#12
Princess Anne

#2
Prince William

#5
Prince Henry

#13
Peter Phillips

#16
Zara Phillips

#3
Prince George

#4
Princess Charlotte

#14
Savannah Phillips

#15
Isla Phillips

#17
Mia Grace Tinda

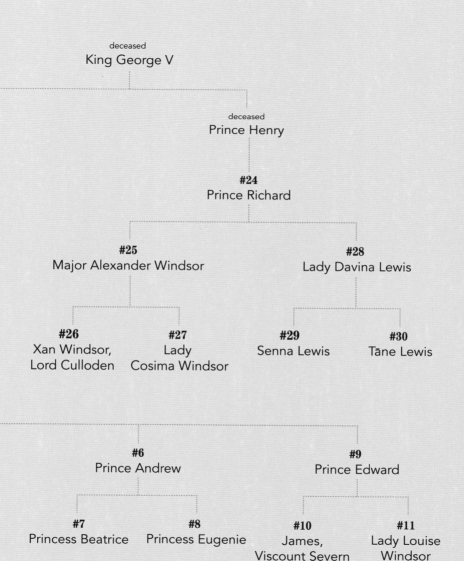

Prince Charles
His Royal Highness
The Prince of Wales

Always the bridesmaid, never the bride, hey, Chuck? Charles Philip Arthur George was born 14 November 1948 at Buckingham Palace, the first grandchild of King George VI and son of Queen Elizabeth II. He has been the first in line to the throne since before the invention of the colour television. Now, that's quite a wait.

Career and first marriage

After spending his formative years frolicking about taking arts courses at Cambridge and playing battleships in the Navy, Charlie eventually settled down, hitching his wagon to none other than the ebullient and beautiful Lady Diana Spencer. But the births of their two young princes, William and Harry, weren't enough to keep the royal couple together and after a flurry of indiscretions, the two divorced in 1996.

In the interim

In the public eye Charles has always strived to remain a symbol of youth and vitality. Being voted World's Best Dressed Man by *Esquire* magazine and having his bum pinched by Ginger Spice went a long way to secure this much esteemed standing in society.

When he's not being the kind of sex symbol Chuck Norris could never be, Charlie spends his time in-wait painting watercolour self-portraits, in the hope that if his lineage never comes to fruition, at least future generations will be aware of his existence.

Current status

Today, Charles is perhaps best known for being Lady Di's ex. His current marriage to Camilla Parker-Bowles is a conundrum we just can't get our heads around. "Come on, Charlie, you were married to the Princess of Wales for crying out loud! You can't do better than that, mate."

When he's not doting on the Duchess of Cornwall, Prince Charles is bending the ears of cabinet ministers in order to lobby interest into pet causes such as the therapeutic benefits of conversing with plant life.

If he was King

At this point it seems unlikely he ever will be, which is probably why he paints his own portraits. But, if for a moment, we could imagine a King Charles III, the world might be a pretty nice place. Like the other kings before him, he'd probably just be your typical polo-playing charisma factory who doesn't mind making the occasional appearance on Jimmy Fallon.

Fast Facts

LINEAGE: The 21st Prince of Wales

MARRIED TO: Camilla Parker-Bowles

CHILDREN: Prince William, Prince Henry

SCHOOL: Eton College

UNIVERSITY: Cambridge

CAREER: Navy

DEFINING FEATURE: Ears

LIKES: Wide-leg trousers

DISLIKES: Cats

UNIQUE SKILLS: Helicopter piloting

ACHIEVEMENTS: Wrote the children's book *The Old Man of Lochnagar* in 1980. Voted World's Best Dressed Man by *Esquire* magazine in 2009.

TELEVISION APPEARANCES: Wrote and hosted the 1988 documentary *A Vision of Britain*; appeared in the 40th Anniversary of *Coronation Street*

REGRET: Turned down a role in *Doctor Who*

HOBBIES: Watercolouring, hedgelaying

MUSIC: Prince, Leonard Cohen, The Corrs

MOVIE: *Purple Rain*

LITTLE-KNOWN FACT: In 1975 he spent 47 minutes underwater examining the wreck of a Tudor warship

OMG: Was called sexy and had his bottom pinched by Ginger Spice of The Spice Girls

SPORTS: Polo and skiing

SOCIAL CONCERNS: Environment

BUSINESS VENTURES: Launched his own food company in 1992 named Duchy Originals. They sell wheat biscuits … delicious!

RITE OF PASSAGE: Given an Aston Martin on his 21st birthday

BEVERAGE: Wheatgrass juice

SAY WHAT?: Charles holds curtseying competitions. Whoever bows the lowest, wins

HOW RICH?: Owns over 130,000 acres of land

TRAVEL: Didn't 'officially' visit the United States until 1994

POWER PLAY: In 2000 he reintroduced the title of Official Harpist to The Prince Of Wales

Prince William

His Royal Highness
The Duke of Cambridge

William Arthur Philip Louis Windsor was born 21 June 1982. (Unlike his father, he was born in a hospital. How common!) While members of his immediate family apparently call him 'Wombat', Big Willie is more than likely to be coroneted one day in the not too distant future. So we ought to take him seriously.

Early life

After being reared by parents whose lives were more complex and dramatic than a good episode of *Neighbours*, Little Willie developed interests in biology and geography (yawn). He would go on to pursue these subjects at Eton College before boldly embarking on a 'gap yah' in order to serve the crown in an army training exercise as a dairy farmer in Belize.

Family

"He may not have inherited his father's ears, but at least he's balding prematurely." This is a direct quote, taken from an awestruck Kate Middleton during her first date with Prince William back in 2003. It was love at first sight, apparently, which is why the two weren't married until 2011. Since that time the pair have produced an heir and an heiress to the throne – George and Charlotte.

Current status

Today, William is a keen airman, having worked as an operational pilot at RAF Valley in North Wales. He is currently a full-time pilot in the East Anglian Air Ambulance service based near Cambridge. Encouraged by his younger brother, Harry, Wills sometimes likes to close UK airports so that he can play air-chicken with university chums, leaving Kate to attend to the nappies.

When he's not piloting his own craft through the skies, he practises emerging from private jets while buttoning his blazer one-handed. Just like his idol, James Bond.

If he was King

Even before William's posterior shuffles into position on the throne, he will have borrowed from North Korea and implemented a mandatory male hairstyle. No man will be allowed to grow more hair than His Highness, and failure to adhere to this rule will result in the laser removal of one's entire head – a potentially unpopular move, but one that will at least help keep the global population in check.

Fast Facts

NICKNAMES: Big Willie, P. Willie, Wills, Billy, Wombat, Prince of Wails

LINEAGE: Descendant of Elimar I, Count of Oldenburg

FATHER: Charles, Prince of Wales

MOTHER: Diana, Princess of Wales

CHILDREN: Prince George, Princess Charlotte

SCHOOL: Eton College

UNIVERSITY: St Andrews

RELATIONSHIP: Married to Catherine Middleton

RELIGION: Church of England

CAREER: Helicopter pilot

DEFINING FEATURE: Baldness

IDENTIFYING MARK: Forehead was hit by a golf club, leaving a 'Harry Potter' style scar

LIKES: Hats

DISLIKES: Hair-based discrimination

REGRET: Wearing onesies as a child

FOOD: Banana flan

DRINK: Stella Artois, Sambuca shots

HOBBIES: Skiing, tennis, soccer, hockey, rafting, rowing, shooting

SONG: *I Like The Way You Move* by The Bodyrockers; anything by Justin Bieber

MOVIE: *Goldfinger*

BOOK: The Jason Steed series

FOOTBALL TEAM: Aston Villa

CHILDHOOD CRUSH: Pamela Anderson

LITTLE-KNOWN FACT: Miranda Kerr and Eva Longoria have publicly revealed their fondness for Will

OMG: Roughly 2 billion people tuned in to watch his wedding

SPORTS: (see Hobbies)

SOCIAL CONCERNS: Animal welfare, homelessness, women's rights, mountain rescue

PATRONAGE: Tusk Trust, Centrepoint

CHARITABLE VENTURES: Donates his annual salary to the Air Ambulance Charity

HOW RICH?: Donates his annual salary to the Air Ambulance Charity

RITE OF PASSAGE: Qualified as a search and rescue pilot; saved an injured man on a mountain in stormy weather

TRAVEL: New Zealand to partake in WWII commemorations

POWER PLAY: Marrying Catherine Middleton, improving his public image one-hundred-fold

Prince George

His Royal Highness
Prince George of Cambridge

George Alexander Louis arrived into the world only a few short years ago on 22 July 2013. Little George heads a new generation of royals who might grow up closer to their publicists than their parents. But then, maybe he'll grow tired of our media-saturated environment and retreat to one of his many castles to lead a life committed to conservatism, abstinence and tradition.

Early life

We all remember our first six months, right? That immersive cacophony of clicks and whirls as the paparazzi took our pictures. It's a dark time for many a young lad – attention hungry, obsessed with public image and reckless experience, your face on the cover of *Vanity Fair*. Like all of us, such was the path for George.

The Prince George effect

Tabloid-obsessed consumers covet everything the boy touches, wears, gushes over or giggles at, which would be quite a burden for us mere mortals. But the G-man shoulders the burden of dictating toddler styles the world over with ease. His panache has been noted by other young celebs, including the Pinkett-Smiths and the Beckhams.

Stuffed-animal addiction

According to reports there is, however, a more sinister side to George. As of late, Little G has regressed into a debilitating stuffed-animal addiction. The accumulated toys donated by presidents and prime ministers across the globe have become an overwhelming fixation in the young man's life and, as of present, George remains hidden beneath a mound of bears, giraffes and cats, protesting a lack of ice cream in his life.

Some people even say that George converses with his stuffed animals as if they were real, but those people know nothing of the unsettling realities of childhood stardom.

If he was King

King George is likely to crawl one path: after graduating from Eton he'll agree to appear on Oprah and become a staunch advocate of conservative parenting. He'll implement an 18+ age restriction on the sale of mobile phones, cameras and the internet, and ban the sale of cuddly toys. He'll also denounce his 'hipster phase' in favour of comfortable slacks and a razor.

Fast Facts

NICKNAMES: Georgie, G-man, Little G

LINEAGE: Descends from the two illegitimate sons of King Charles II – Henry FitzRoy and Charles Lennox

FATHER: Prince William

MOTHER: Catherine Middleton

CHILDREN: None as yet

SCHOOL: Eton College, most probably

RELATIONSHIP: Enamoured with the royal slinky

RELIGION: Church of England

CAREER: Still figuring things out

DEFINING FEATURE: Baby fat

LIKES: Stuffed animals

DISLIKES: Low-quality caviar

REGRET: Failing to take time to smell the roses

HOBBIES: Stuffed-animal enthusiast

ACHIEVEMENTS: Appeared in colour on the cover of *Vanity Fair* before he could see in colour

BOOK: *Everybody Burps Politely*

MUSIC: *Royals* by Lorde

MOVIE: *Gone Baby Gone*

OMG: His first scandal was appearing on the cover of *US Weekly*, heavily retouched

SPORT: Long-distance regurgitation

SOCIAL CONCERNS: Ageism

FAME: The Prince George Effect (or Royal Baby Effect), whereby products and clothing used by George sell better than those that aren't

CHARITABLE VENTURE: Recycling of nappies

RITE OF PASSAGE: Heavily publicised Royal Christening

HOW RICH?: In October 2013, coins were made in honour of his christening, each worth £80,000

TRAVEL: Carried around Australia and New Zealand

POWER PLAY: First-born child

INFLUENCES: North West, Blue Ivy Carter

INFLUENCED: Princess Charlotte of Cambridge, Saint West

TRUE STORY: The Prince once pretended his legs weren't working so that his father was forced to carry the boy on his shoulders. Makes one wonder who's really in charge down there in Cambridge.

Princess Charlotte

Her Royal Highness
Princess Charlotte of Cambridge

C harlotte Elizabeth Diana was born 2 May 2015 to the Duke and Duchess of Cambridge. Not many of us have landmarks lit in our honour, nor do we receive gun salutes, but within two days the Princess had both, as per her request.

Born to rule

If she's to take after her mother in any way then Her Royal Highness could probably get away with wearing tracksuit pants with the words 'born to rule' displayed across the backside in cursive and every American would be hitting the shops the next day to don the same outfit. But, thankfully, her mother has a little more class than this, so Charlotte might just be the most glorious of second-wave Middleton fashionistas.

Role models

Young Charlotte has a lot to live up to. Her grandmother's death stopped the world, and the outpouring of emotion during this event demonstrated the magnitude of Diana's effect on us all. Her mother has already left her mark – it's called the 'Kate Middleton effect' – and while perhaps a little less complicated than the mark left by the passing of Lady Di, you can't ignore the power of a person who causes others to undergo cosmetic surgery in their likeness.

Like brother, like sister

It has been noted, however, that Charlotte appears to be afflicted with the same condition as her elder brother, George. That's right, like the G Star, little Lottie has been gravitating towards the addictive comfort of plush toys and demanding more easily digestible soft foods, such as puréed truffles.

If she was Queen

A future with Charlotte at the helm is a bright one. Currently she seems a little apathetic about her future role, sure, but whenever she smiles the rest of us can't help smiling too. Put her in charge!

No, no, scratch that. If you're listening Royals, that was a joke. Don't put her in charge, she's a baby. It would be, like, a really, really bad idea.

Fast Facts

NICKNAMES: Lottie, Baby Girl

LINEAGE: A descendant of Prince Philip – unfortunately, there are some relatives the Royals just can't shake

FATHER: Prince William, Duke of Cambridge

MOTHER: Catherine Middleton, Duchess of Cambridge

TALENT: Licking spoons

SCHOOL: Life

RELATIONSHIP: Teddy bear

RELIGION: Church of England

DEFINING FEATURE: Most powerful baby in the world

LIKES: Unicorns

DISLIKES: Unicorn hunters (they're a thing, they're real, they exist; Charlotte just doesn't understand the true meaning of the term, yet)

ACHIEVEMENTS: Most powerful baby in the world

REGRET: Being the second-born child

HOBBIES: Chewing on stuff

FOOD: Chewed-up stuff

DRINK: Mother's milk with a splash of gin

BOOK: *The Jungle Book*

SONG: *The Bare Necessities*

MOVIE: *The Jungle Book 2*

SOCIAL CONCERNS: Unicorns and their potential extinction

CHARITABLE VENTURES: Smiling at her mother and father

RITE OF PASSAGE: Having Tower Bridge, the London Eye and the fountains in Trafalgar Square illuminated pink in honour of her birth

LITTLE-KNOWN FACT: Has atheist leanings after dropping her teddy bear in the church font

OMG: People fired rifles at the Tower of London and Hyde Park because Lottie made them so pleased

TRAVEL: Currently planning a gap year between kindergarten and big school

POWER PLAY: Has taken George's favourite cuddly toy and made it her own

FAVOURITE COLOUR: Pink

Prince Henry

His Royal Highness
Prince Henry of Wales

Henry Charles Albert David was born 15 September 1984 and, for no reason at all, immediately changed his name to Harry. Once the third in line to the throne, Harry has moved down the pecking order with the births of his nephew and niece.

A rebel without a charitable cause

After dealing with the sudden passing of his mother at age 12, graduating from Eton in 2003, and taking a gap year in Australia where he played polo and worked on a cattle station, Prince Harry soon became embroiled in many a tabloid scandal.

Such indignities included a short stay at a rehabilitation clinic at the behest of Prince Charles for smoking a doob; putting up his dukes to go toe-to-toe with a paparazzo; and wearing a Nazi uniform to a costume party.

Currently

In recent years, Harry has tried to shed his image as the royal party animal, but this might just be an attempt to polish his public persona. For all we know, he's still playing strip billiards and sexting like mad behind closed doors. In fact, most of us secretly hope he still is.

The real deal

Despite his public misdemeanours, the fact remains that Harry is the first royal to see military action since Prince Andrew in 1981. And the man can fly a helicopter, for Pete's sake. Cut him some slack!

Oh, and let's not forget his humanitarian work, for which he has received two awards: a Golden Heart Award and a Distinguished Humanitarian Leadership Award. That's right, between flying choppers, fighting in war zones, and taking his clothes off in pool halls, the prince somehow finds the time to give back to a legion of worthy causes, most notably those concerning children in need and wounded soldiers.

If he was King

One day England may wake up and realise their King is an army combatant whose first loves are rugby and polo. Oh yeah, and he doesn't mind women, whiskey and weed, either. It'd be just like the old times …

Fast Facts

NICKNAME: Harry, Spike, My Little Spencer

LINEAGE: Descendant of Elimar I, Count of Oldenburg

FATHER: Charles, Prince of Wales

MOTHER: Diana, Princess of Wales

CHILDREN: None, that he is aware of

CHILDHOOD TALENT: Snatching the limelight from his older brother

SCHOOL: Eton College

RELIGION: Church of England

FORMER CAREER: Pilot

CAREER HIGHLIGHTS: Promoted to Lieutenant in 2008; ended service after a decade

FUTURE CAREER: Charity or public service

DEFINING FEATURE: A passing resemblance to James Hewitt

LIKES: Studying flowers

DISLIKES: Commitment

ACHIEVEMENTS: Produced the AIDS documentary *The Forgotten Kingdom*

REGRET: Getting caught

HOBBIES: Strip billiards

FOOD: Fried chicken, pizza, chocolate

DRINK: Orange soda and Coca Cola

MUSIC: Dubstep, Reggae, Miley Cyrus

MOVIES: *Full Metal Jacket, Black Hawk Down, Platoon*

CAR: Aston Martin (shared with Will)

SPORTS: Rugby, skiing, horsing around on horses

FOOTBALL TEAM: Arsenal

SOCIAL CONCERNS: AIDS, child welfare

PATRONAGE: Twelve charities including MapAction, Dolen Cymru, Walking with the Wounded and WellChild

CHARITABLE VENTURE: Asked that all money made from the sale of his 18th birthday photo go to charity

RITE OF PASSAGE: The first Royal to see military action since Prince Andrew in 1981

LITTLE-KNOWN FACT: The Taliban targeted Prince Harry while he was stationed in Afghanistan

OMG: Harry has turned out to be better looking than his brother

TRAVEL: Cattle station in Australia, South Pole, Africa

POWER PLAY: He quit the military after a decade to stay in closer proximity to the throne.

FAVOURITE COLOUR: Orange

Prince Andrew

His Royal Highness
The Duke of York

A British prince since birth, Andrew Albert Christian Edward came into the world on 19 February 1960. He was baptised in Buckingham Palace's music room.

Early life and career

Like many of the Royals, Andy spent time fluttering about in the navy and learning to pilot helicopters. But unlike many of the Royals today (Prince Harry being the exception) the Duke of York saw combat. Serving as a helicopter co-pilot, he flew on missions during the Falklands War, which included, among other things, search and air rescue, transportation and casualty evacuation, and anti-submarine and anti-surface warfare. Now, that's the real deal.

Relationships

In 1986, Andrew married Sarah Ferguson. While the marriage wasn't particularly joyous, the two managed to produce two daughters – Beatrice and Eugenie. And although many argue that it was Fergie's infidelity that's to be blamed for the disintegration of their marriage, some sources believe it was Andrew's appetite for the illicit that pushed her away.

Controversy

We'll never really know what The Grand Old Duke of York gets up to behind closed doors. While there have been many, many rumours, the allegations made against his character have been conveniently struck from the public record. Ah, the benefits of being a Royal! However, Andy's friendships with the likes of Jeffrey Epstein and Ilham Aliyev have certainly raised many an eyebrow.

If he was King

King Andy, now there's a thought. A deeply troubling one, many might say. Who knows how much he might lower the age of consent, or how many nuclear arms deals he would make with dictators. Thankfully, the chance of Prince Andrew's rise to monarchic power is no more than a glint in his wandering eye.

Fast Facts

FULL NAME: His Royal Highness The Prince Andrew Albert Christian Edward, Duke of York, Earl of Inverness, Baron Killyleagh, Knight Companion of the Most Noble Order of the Garter, Knight Grand Cross of the Royal Victorian Order, Canadian Forces Decoration, Aide-de-Camp to Her Majesty

NICKNAME: Randy Andy

FATHER: Prince Phillip, Duke of Edinburgh

MOTHER: Queen Elizabeth II

CHILDREN: Princess Beatrice of York, Princess Eugenie of York

SCHOOL: Gordonstoun, Scotland

RELATIONSHIP: Sarah Ferguson (1986–96); others that the public is not privy to

RELIGION: Church of England

CAREER: Full-time Royal – UK Department of Trade and Industry

ACHIEVEMENTS: Commodore of the Royal Yacht Club; trustee of the National Maritime Museum; first Royal to set up a Twitter account

DEFINING FEATURE: Long arms

LIKES: Rich people

DISLIKES: Rules

HOBBIES: THIS SENTENCE HAS BEEN REMOVED BY THE OFFICE OF THE ROYAL FAMILY

BOOK: *Lolita*

MOVIE: *Free Willy*

LITTLE-KNOWN FACT: First born to a reigning monarch since Queen Victoria's youngest daughter, Beatrice

CONTROVERSY: Accused of using his position to promote arms sales

LOL: Gave the Vulcan salute to Patrick Stewart

OMG: Friends with Jeffrey Epstein

SPORTS: Squash, hockey, golf, hide the sausage

SOCIAL CONCERNS: Education, science and engineering

PATRONAGE: More than one Royal golf club

CHARITABLE VENTURES: Fight For Sight, Attend

RITE OF PASSAGE: Fergie

TRAVEL: All corners of the globe promoting British business, preferably on yachts

POWER PLAY: A highly suspicious friendship with the president of Azerbaijan

Princess Beatrice

Her Royal Highness Princess Beatrice Elizabeth Mary of York

Born 8 August 1988, Beatrice Elizabeth Mary is the first daughter of Sarah Ferguson and Prince Andrew. Luckily for Bea, this date is considered lucky in Chinese numerology and a sign that her life will be filled with wealth and prosperity. Who would have thought?

Early life and education

Beatrice attended St. George's School in Ascot, where she was immediately elected 'Head Girl' and studied drama, history and film studies. After finishing school, she spent time volunteering with noble organisations such as Selfridges Department Store. She then went on to graduate from the University of London with a degree in history and history of ideas.

Hats

Despite her education, Beatrice upheaved her career path, channelling her energies into the lost craft of high-end millinery. She spends most of her time tracking down the rarest and most elaborate headpieces, or having her dream hat custom made. To Beatrice, nothing is more fascinating than a striking fascinator; wordplay that some say she proudly claims to have coined.

Hats, part II

At the Royal Wedding in 2011, Beatrice took her fondness for headgear to new heights, matching her dusty pink garment with a Lewis Carroll-esque hat that resembled both an oversized doorknocker and an octopus. Though this stylistic choice received much criticism from the general public, Beatrice has remained strident, and is standing as upright as possible.

If she was Queen

The first order of business for Queen Bea will be a complete stylistic overhaul. From princes to peasants, everybody will be given the type of makeover they've only dreamed about. Unfortunately, though, every doorway in England will have to be altered to make room for the new hats and garments.

Fast Facts

NICKNAME: The Mad Hatter

FATHER: Prince Andrew, Duke of York

MOTHER: Sarah, Duchess of York

SCHOOL: St. George's School

UNIVERSITY: University of London

RELATIONSHIP: Dave Clark

RELIGION: Church of England

CAREER: Currently unemployed

CAREER HIGHLIGHTS: Appearing as an extra in *The Young Victoria* (2009)

DEFINING FEATURE: Hats

LIKES: Hats

DISLIKES: Cats in hats

FOOD: Corn on the cob

HOBBIES: Hats; holidays

BOOKS: The Harry Potter series

MOVIES: The Harry Potter series

MUSIC: BBC Radio 1

LITTLE-KNOWN FACT: In 2015, Beatrice enjoyed a total of 15 separate holidays after leaving her job at Sony

OMG: Spent £300,000 on holidays in one year

PET PEEVE: Children in crisis

SOCIAL CONCERNS: Getting a tan

CHARITABLE VENTURES: Royal patron of the Helen Arkell Dyslexia Centre

RITE OF PASSAGE: Taking as many flights in one year as most people average in a lifetime

HOW RICH?: Claiming the royal equivalent of the dole

TRAVEL: Wherever she likes, whenever she likes – she's a princess, God dammit!

FAVOURITE COLOUR: Orange

INFLUENCES: Paris Hilton, Kim Kardashian

INFLUENCED: Pixie Geldof

DEFINING FEATURE: An overwhelming sense of entitlement

TRADEMARK: Lounging on boats

PRAISE: Her mother has said young Beatrice is financially savvy. Well, she must be if she can afford all those holidays.

NEPOTISM: "Pardon?"

Princess Eugenie

Her Royal Highness Princess Eugenie Victoria Helena of York

Born 23 March 1990, Eugenie Victoria Helena is the second daughter of the Duke and Duchess of York, and the sixth grandchild of Queen Elizabeth II.

Early years

Eugenie's parents divorced when she was just six years old. When she was twelve, she underwent invasive surgery to correct her scoliosis, which involved two titanium rods being put into her back. Despite these setbacks, Eugenie managed to see out her years at boarding school and go on to graduate from Newcastle University in 2012.

Career

In 2013, Eugenie moved to New York City where she worked for a year as a benefit auctions manager for an online auction firm. More recently, she has continued her work in the art world as an associate director of an art gallery back home in London.

Unlike other Royals, the Princess does not represent the Royal Family in official duties and she receives no money from the royal bank account. Although she does attend some royal engagements, Eugenie's pretty down to earth, preferring instead to pursue her career and, like a lot of young women, attend Beyoncé concerts.

Current status

Prin-E spends much of her time these days throwing themed parties and painting her nails for the other themed parties she's forced to attend. (She sported reindeers on her fingernails at last year's Christmas party in Buckingham Palace). But despite the pizzazz she's been flaunting on her digits lately, Eugenie can't compete with her sister's array of fascinators and she knows it.

If she was Queen

Much like her sister, if Prin-E ever became Queen-E, we would probably see quite a shake-up in the fashion stakes. Hats, of course, would be outlawed and redheads everywhere would be forced to spend their lives indoors and out of sight as a result. Oh, and she'd improve the lives of a lot of young people who really deserve it, too.

Fast Facts

NICKNAMES: Eugene; Jeanie; Ewwww-genie

FATHER: Prince Andrew, Duke of York

MOTHER: Sarah, Duchess of York

SCHOOL: Marlborough College Boarding School

UNIVERSITY: Newcastle University

DEGREE: English literature, history of art and politics

RELATIONSHIP: Jack Brooksbank (on and off since 2010)

RELIGION: Church of England

CAREER: Fine art world

CAREER HIGHLIGHTS: Benefit Auction Manager for Paddle8 in NYC

DEFINING FEATURE: Not being a redhead

LIKES: Art

DISLIKES: Hats

FOOD: Pickled Onion Monster Munch

FILM APPEARANCE: *The Duchess in Hull* (documentary)

HOBBIES: Hosting themed parties

BOOK: *Fifty Shades of Grey*

MOVIE: *Fast and Furious 3*

MUSIC: Beyoncé

LITTLE-KNOWN FACT: Had two titanium rods inserted into her back in order to correct her scoliosis

OMG: While in the front row of a Beyoncé concert, she was approached by the singer and encouraged to sing into the microphone

PET PEEVE: The attention surrounding her sister's hats

HOBBIES: Karaoke

SOCIAL CONCERNS: Improving the lives of young people with cancer

CHARITABLE VENTURES: Teenage Cancer Trust

RITE OF PASSAGE: Parents divorced when she was six

HOW RICH?: Although she receives no money from the privy purse, it's safe to assume she has enough to scrape by

TRAVEL: London to NY, NY to London

POWER PLAY: Called Granny, "truly one of the most amazing women ever. All I can say is she has this air of magic about her."

Prince Edward

His Royal Highness The Earl of Wessex

Edward Anthony Richard Louis was born 10 March 1964. At the time he was third in line to the throne, but since the births of his nephews and nieces and their children too, poor old Ed has slipped down the list to ninth place. Drats!

The runt of the litter

The fourth and youngest child of Queen Elizabeth II, Andrew was always a little bit special. From a young age he was determined to strike out on his own, but the looming shadow of the Royal Family can at times be a stifling one. Despite an underwhelming academic record he somehow managed to get into Cambridge, where he graduated with lower second-class honours before attempting and failing twice to pursue careers away from the Royals.

Non-Royal career (first attempt)

After completing just one-third of a 12-month-long commando training course, Andrew dropped out of the Royal Marines. But to be fair, it was really, really hard.

And so began his first big mission in life: a career in theatrical production. Cleverly enough he took hold of the tailcoats of Andrew Lloyd-Webber and Tim Rice, holding on with both hands as they ascended the theatrical ladder, but it was to little avail. He spent most of his time in live theatre making tea for the staff and dating one of the actresses.

Non-Royal career (second attempt)

Eddie's next foray into the arts, would be in television. In 1987, he produced a game show called *The Grand Knockout Tournament* in which the Earl, Princess Anne and Prince Andrew each sponsored a team of celebrities, who faced slapstick challenges in the name of charity. The Queen was not impressed. It was apparent that Eddie was already becoming dependent on his Royal connections, a trend he would continue with the formation of Ardent Productions in 1993, where he made documentaires about other members of the Royal Family. The business went bust in 2009 and Ed returned to Royal duties with his tail between his legs.

If he was King

With Edward at the helm the world might just get what it's been dreaming of: Buckingham.com – a live-streaming website showing every royal movement, bowels and all.

Fast Facts

NICKNAMES: Edward Teaspoonhands

FATHER: Prince Phillip, Duke of Edinburgh

MOTHER: Queen Elizabeth II

CHILDREN: Lady Louise Windsor; James, Viscount Severn

SCHOOL: Gordonstoun, Scotland

UNIVERSITY: Cambridge

RELATIONSHIP: Sophie Rhys-Jones

RELIGION: Church of England

DEFINING FEATURE: Signature royal male-pattern baldness

CAREER: After dropping out of the Royal Marines and the entertainment industry, he became a full-time member of the Royal Family

LIKES: Theatrical production

DISLIKES: Theatrical production

REGRET: Dropping from third in line to the throne all the way to ninth

HOBBIES: Prank-calling Andrew-Lloyd Webber

BOOK: *Television Production for Dummies*

MUSIC: Musicals

MOVIE: *The Queen*

SPORT: Commissioned the musical *Cricket* for Andrew Lloyd Webber and Tim Rice

LITTLE-KNOWN FACT: In what was definitely NOT the result of nepotism, he won the Gold Duke of Edinburgh Award in 1986

OMG: Created the much maligned television show *The Grand Knockout Tournament*, where royals battled for charity alongside the likes of Meat Loaf, John Travolta, John Cleese and Christopher Reeve.

CONTROVERSY: Was admitted to Cambridge despite sub-par entry grades

SOCIAL CONCERNS: Young people

CHARITABLE VENTURES: Involved with over 75 charitable organisations (he has to do something with his time)

HOW RICH?: Still receives pocket money from Mummy and Daddy

TRAVEL: New Zealand

POWER PLAY: Selflessly sacrificing his career in the entertainment industry to better serve the crown

QUOTE: On his wedding (not his wedding night): "It was great fun and over far too quickly."

James, Viscount Severn

Lord Severn

The youngest grandchild of Queen Elizabeth II, James Alexander Philip Theo Mountbatten-Windsor was born December 17 2007 to Prince Edward, Earl of Wessex, and Sophie, Countess of Wessex.

Pastimes

With a dad like Ed, Jimmy could be forgiven for not coming to appreciate the art of the hunt. In 2014 a photo emerged of James' father shooting a rifle over his son's head. But despite this incident, young James doesn't mind joining his mother, father and older sister on trips to Sandringham to fire at pheasants. It's just your typical family weekend away.

Career

When he's not avoiding rifle shots or finding coded patterns within obscure Latin texts, Buckingham insiders claim that behind closed doors, James, Viscount Severn displays some troubling tendencies. He is known to appear out of thin air in random nooks and crannies around the palace whispering to guards, "If my sister comes by, pretend I'm not here, okay?" The Queen herself has several times awoken in the middle of the night to find James in the kitchen atop a stepladder reaching for the higher shelves in the pantry.

Future

With continued trips to Sandringham, James' marksmanship is sure to improve. We see him one day completing that commando course his father quit in 1987.

If he was King

Should King James take the throne today it may be a period marked by his escalating eccentricity. The eight-year-old will bring back the jesters of yesteryear while administering strange new rules: those who can't reach the top shelves of the pantry will be forced to traverse the length of the palace while balancing on a roll of 50p coins. You know, kids' stuff.

Fast Facts

NICKNAME: Jimmy Discount

FATHER: Prince Edward, Earl of Wessex

MOTHER: Sophie, Countess of Wessex

CHILDHOOD: Spent dodging bullets

RELIGION: Church of England

RESIDES: Bagshot Park, Surrey

SCHOOL: The royal knee

RELATIONSHIP: Remote-control Range Rovers

HOBBIES: Hiding

DEFINING FEATURE: Rarely seen in public, leaving his features open for speculation

LIKES: When Granny plays dead to make the family laugh

DISLIKES: When Granny plays dead to make the family laugh but the family grow excited

FOOD: Chocolate biscuits

TV APPEARANCE: The 2011 Royal Wedding

REGRET: The fact a comma follows his first name

BOOK: *Little Lord Fauntleroy*

MOVIE: *One Flew Over The Cuckoo's Nest*

MUSIC: The Wiggles (but only their early stuff)

LITTLE-KNOWN FACT: Was born at 4.20 pm, which has the pro-marijuana population giggling

OMG: Is a moderator for a Reddit subreddit on childhood anxiety

RITE OF PASSAGE: The result of a caesarean section

TRAVEL: First international trip to South Africa in 2015

FAVOURITE COLOUR: Camouflage khaki

ACTION HERO: Wolverine

INFLUENCES: Willow Smith

INFLUENCED: Cousin George

TRUE STORY: James was the first Royal child to wear an exact replica of the christening gown originally worn by his great-great-great-grand-aunt Victoria, Princess Royal, Queen Victoria's eldest daughter

PRAISE: The papers reported that directly after the birth of his son, Prince Edward said he was "like most babies, rather small, very cute and very cuddly." That's high praise, Dad!

BESTIE: Pope Francis. They share the same birthday

Lady Louise Windsor

Louise Alice Elizabeth Mary Mountbatten-Windsor was born prematurely on 8 November 2003. Her arrival into the world of the Royals was a dramatic and rather unexpected one, which meant that her father was not present to witness the occasion. Poor old Ed. It's a bit of a theme, isn't it?

A man's world

Unlike her cousin, Charlotte, Lady Louise was not able to reap the benefits of the changes to succession law that were effected in 2015 and so, despite being the eldest child in the family, the birth of her younger brother, James, displaced her in succession to the throne. Damn those sexist traditions!

Early hardships

Born with esotropia (a condition in which one or both eyes turn inwards), Louise underwent surgery in 2006 and 2013 to correct her vision.

If she was Queen

It's likely that Louise would've gone on to make those changes to succession law that benefitted her cousin, had they not been enacted in 2015. From all accounts nothing gets a young lady riled up quite so much as seeing little brothers leapfrog their sisters to power. Should Lou ever make it to the throne, she will become a staunch feminist, enforcing equal pay for women throughout the Commonwealth.

Fast Facts

NICKNAME: Louise Alice Elizabeth Mary Mountbatten-Windsor

LINEAGE: Her mother is descended from King Henry IV of England

FATHER: Prince Edward, Earl of Wessex

MOTHER: Sophie, Countess of Wessex

CHILDREN: One day, but let's not rush the poor girl

UNIVERSITY: One day, one day, settle down!

RELATIONSHIP: Kermit the Frog

RELIGION: Church of England

LIKES: Shortbread biscuits

DISLIKES: Little boys

MUSIC: Disney classics

SOCIAL CONCERNS: Gender politics

PASSIONATE ABOUT: Feminism

TRAVEL: Accompanied her mother and father on a visit to South Africa

CAREER HIGHLIGHT: Louise was a bridesmaid at the wedding of the Duke and Duchess of Cambridge

TROUBLING SIGNS: Reported to be trying to take down her brother from the inside

OMG: Goes pheasant shooting. She's a little girl!

RITE OF PASSAGE: Sustained an injury mucking about on horses – it's a Royal thing

COLOUR: Pastels

Fast Facts

FULL TITLE: Her Royal Highness The Princess Anne Elizabeth Alice Louise, Princess Royal, Royal Lady of the Most Noble Order of the Garter, Extra Lady of the Most Ancient and Most Noble Order of the Thistle, Dame Grand Cross and Grand Master of the Royal Victorian Order, Dame Grand Cross of the Most Venerable Order of the Hospital of St. John of Jerusalem

FATHER: Prince Philip, Duke of Edinburgh

MOTHER: Queen Elizabeth II

SCHOOL: Benenden School

RELATIONSHIPS: Captain Mark Phillips (1973–1992); Sir Timothy Laurence (1992–)

RELIGION: Church of England

SPORT: Equestrian

MOVIES: *Black Beauty, Seabiscuit*

MUSIC: *F*@# tha Police*, NWA

LIKES: Fast cars

DISLIKES: Horse burgers

FOOD: Beef vindaloo

TRAVEL: In Anne's book there's no better place to be than cruising down that dual carriageway, pedal to the metal

Princess Anne

Her Royal Highness The Princess Royal

Anne Elizabeth Alice Louise was born 15 August 1950 at Clarence House, the second child of Queen Elizabeth II and Prince Philip, Duke of Edinburgh. Like Lady Louise, Anne was displaced in line to the throne by the births of her two younger brothers, Andrew and Edward.

Marriages

In 1973, Anne married Captain Mark Phillips. The couple had two children, Peter and Zara, but would ultimately divorce in 1992. That same year Anne married Sir Timothy Laurence, and the two remain together today.

Kidnapping attempt

In 1974, a man named Ian Ball attempted to kidnap the princess. Ball shot and injured Anne's personal police officer, her chauffeur, and a nearby tabloid journalist who tried to intervene. Fortunately, nobody was killed.

If she was Queen

Anne has had a couple of clashes with the law. She was once charged for speeding on a dual carriageway, and fined under the Dangerous Dogs Act of 1991 when her pet dog Dotty attacked two children. It is, therefore, safe to assume that monarchic rule under Queen Anne would see the abolishment of speed limits and the creation of dog-fighting syndicates outside the walls of Buck Palace.

Peter Phillips

Peter Mark Andrew Phillips was born 15 November 1977 to parents Mark Phillips and Anne, Princess Royal. He is Anne's only son and the Queen's oldest grandchild.

Lack of official royal title

Back in 1973 Peter's father, Mark, made a bit of a statement. As an untitled man marrying into the Royal family it is customary for one to take something called an 'earldom'. But, on his wedding day, having been offered said peerage by Queen Elizabeth II, Mark turned it down.

When Peter was born the Queen again made another offer of peerage and therefore eligibility to a style. But Peter's folks once more said no. The result? Peter was the first grandchild of a monarch to be born without a title in over 500 years. Now, that's better than any title, really.

Career

Like many royal children, Peter attended Gordonstoun School in Scotland, before going on to study at Exeter University where he graduated with a degree in sports science.

Since leaving university, Peter has had a long and successful career in management, working for Jaguar, Williams F1, The Royal Bank of Scotland and, currently, SEL UK.

Fast Facts

NICKNAME: Pee-Pee

FATHER: Captain Mark Phillips

MOTHER: Anne, The Princess Royal

RELATIONSHIP: Autumn Kelly

CHILDREN: Savannah Phillips, Isla Phillips

SCHOOL: Gordonstoun School, Scotland

UNIVERSITY: Exeter

DEFINING FEATURE: Nose

LIKES: Sport

DISLIKES: Embroidery

SPORTS: Formula 1, rugby

LITTLE-KNOWN FACT: Was by his cousin Prince William's side after Lady Di's sudden death

POWER PLAY: Owes his place in the succession line to his wife's conversion from Roman Catholicism to Church of England

RITE OF PASSAGE: Survived a car crash in China in 2004

TALENT: Keeping a low profile and staying out of the press

13

Fast Facts

NICKNAMES: Savvy, Cab Sav, Sav Blanc

FATHER: Peter Phillips

MOTHER: Autumn Phillips

CHILDREN: Hang on a minute

SCHOOL: Eventually, we'll get there

UNIVERSITY: Right, slow down

RELATIONSHIP: Hello Kitty

RELIGION: My Little Pony

BOOK: *The Magic Faraway Tree*

FOOD: Any and all desserts

FILM: *The Lion King*

LIKES: Gallivanting around the open plains of Africa

DISLIKES: Big-game hunting

IDOL: Twilight Sparkle

RITE OF PASSAGE: Hanging out at Windsor Castle and playing chasey with Great Granny

COLOUR: Royal purple

Savannah Phillips

Savannah Anne Kathleen Phillips was born 29 December 2010 and is the first great-granddaughter of Queen Elizabeth II. She is the first child born to Peter and Autumn Phillips. Like her father, Sav has no official royal title.

Life so far

Initial reports indicated a rift between little Savannah and her great-grandmother. The Queen apparently took none-too-kindly to the pointedly un-British first name (literally meaning 'open plains') and the girl's loyalty to her nation was, for a time, called into question.

But fortunately, that's all behind them now, and the two have even been spotted in public together, walking through a garden behind the palace hand-in-hand.

If she was Queen

Ah, Queen Savannah, now there's a title we'd all like to hear. With a name like Sav, this young Royal could just be the kind of ambassador the English people have always hoped for. It would be the beginning of a new age.

Isla Phillips

Isla Elizabeth Phillips was born 29 March 2012, the second daughter of Peter and Autumn Phillips, and one of few Royals to have only three names. Like her father and her older sister, Savannah, Isla is without an official royal title.

Those first four years

We all remember our time spent frolicking about Buckingham Palace, dashing naked through the fountains in Trafalgar Square, and hesitantly petting our grandmother's bull terriers. Well, if not, then that's just a portion of the experiences young Isla has received in her first four years on planet earth.

Who can tell what the next five to ten years will bring for Isla. If she's lucky, she might skip the typical route of elite tertiary education via Gordonstoun followed by a life of heavily planned social engagements and appearances at charitable events. Perhaps, like Beatrice, she'll find herself catching rays on a yacht somewhere nice or maybe, just maybe, she'll do anything else.

If she was Queen

Like her sister, Queen Isla would make for a pretty great title indeed. At this stage perhaps she's a little too young to take the reins, but we can imagine a future in which her grandmother's rogue dogs are muzzled and UGG boots make their way into the palace for the very first time.

Fast Facts

NICKNAMES: I-to-the-P, IPie (pronounced, Ippie)

FATHER: Peter Phillips

MOTHER: Autumn Phillips

EDUCATION: School of life

RELIGION: Church of England

LIKES: Ice cream

DISLIKES: When ice cream melts faster than you can eat it

MOVIE: *Toy Story*

BOOK: *Where the Wild Things Are*

MUSIC: Shoegaze

DEFINING FEATURE: Blonde locks

OMG: Was once spotted secretly planning Great-Granny's downfall

TRAVEL: Womb to the palace

PET PEEVE: Elder sister stealing the limelight

POWER PLAY: Pouts for affection. Alternatively, uses floppy floor tantrums to get own way

IDENTIFYING MARK: Being one of the most adorable children in the world

Fast Facts

FATHER: Mark Phillips

MOTHER: Anne, The Princess Royal

RELATIONSHIP: Mark Tindall

CHILDREN: Mia Tindall

SCHOOL: Gordonstoun School

UNIVERSITY: Exeter

QUALIFICATION: Physiotherapist

CAREER: Horse-related activities; physiotherapy

ACHIEVEMENTS: Eventing World Champion of 2006 through 2010, silver medal in Team Eventing, 2012 London Olympics

LIKES: Riding side-saddle

DISLIKES: Pantomime horses

TRAVEL: Just about everywhere you can imagine, on horseback

SOCIAL CONCERNS: Zara is involved with several charity organisations that target children's causes such as children's cancer and spinal injuries, as well as some equestrian-related charities

OMG: Won a bloody Olympic medal!

FOOD: Carrots

DEFINING FEATURE: Her husband's horrendously broken nose. Seriously, look at Mike Tindall's nose. It's smashed to bits

LITTLE-KNOWN FACT: In 2006, Zara won the BBC Sports Personality of the Year award. Her mother won the same award in 1971

Zara Phillips

Zara Anne Elizabeth Phillips is the second child to Princess Anne and Mark Phillips. She was born 15 May 1981 and holds no royal title.

Life and marriage

Zara is yet another Royal to have attended Gordonstoun School in Scotland. There, she excelled both athletically and academically, before going on to further her studies at Exeter University. She graduated as a qualified physiotherapist.

After meeting English rugby union player Mike Tindall in Australia in 2003, the couple married in 2011. Together they have one child, a daughter, Mia Tindall.

Athletic prowess

We all know the Royals are a horsey lot and Zara is no exception. In fact, she's owned several, all of which have had equally ridiculous and amazing names: Tsunami II, High Kingdom and, our favourite, Toytown.

From 2003, Zara has competed professionally as an equestrian. She has won medals at the 2005 European Eventing Championship, the 2006 FEI World Equestrian Games and the 2007 European Eventing Championship. And in 2012, at the London Olympic Games, Zara won a silver medal in Team Eventing. This occasion was made all the more special by the fact that her own mother, Princess Anne, was the one to present the medal to her star daughter.

Mia Grace Tindall

Mia Grace Tindall was born 17 January 2014 in Gloucester, weighing 7 lbs 12 oz. She is the first and only child to Mike Tindall and Zara Phillips and the third grandchild of Princess Anne. Like her other cousins, Mia has no official royal title.

A year and change

So far Mia has proven to be a rather calm and serene young lady. She isn't fazed by those who mispronounce her name, though we might attribute this to the fact that she hasn't quite fully worked out what it's supposed to sound like either.

Unlike other Royals, Mia has not been seen clashing with other members of the family. There have been little tabloid rumours, no failed marriages, no speeding on freeways or boozy nights out, or revealing photos showing one in stages of undress or waving a rifle above her son's head. No, it's been nice and quiet so far, and we're confident it might stay this way for good. Her folks are some pretty respectable people, after all.

If she was Queen

Were the planets to align and some miraculous turn of events took place putting Mia at the helm, we feel pretty confident for how things in England would pan out. Mia would abolish televisions in the home, turn us all back to active lifestyles and we'd see childhood obesity stamped out for good. Here's hoping Jamie Oliver's ready to step down off his high horse to make room.

Fast Facts

NICKNAME: M (You really can't abbreviate Mia, but sharing a nickname with the head of MI6 is pretty cool)

FATHER: Michael Tindall

MOTHER: Zara Phillips

LIKES: Soft places to lie down on and nap

DISLIKES: Discomfort

RELATIONSHIP: Blankey

RELIGION: Agnostic. She just hasn't found the one for her yet

FOOD: Mushed up stuff. We really don't know what's in it

DRINK: Juice

HOBBIES: Napping

BOOK: *Spot visits the palace*

SONG: Any lullaby will do

MOVIES: Kevin Smith's early films

CHILDHOOD CRUSH: Yet to be developed

DEFINING FEATURE: Being adorable

TALENT: Being adorable

IDENTIFYING MARK: Adorability

Fast Facts

NICKNAMES: Auction Dave, Discount Linley

LINEAGE: Grandson of King George IV

FATHER: Antony Armstrong-Jones, 1st Earl of Snowdon

MOTHER: Princess Margaret, Countess of Snowdon

RELATIONSHIP: Serena Armstrong-Jones, Viscountess Linley

CHILDREN: Charles Armstrong-Jones, Margarita Armstrong-Jones

SCHOOL: Milbrook House

UNIVERSITY: Parnham College

AREA OF STUDY: Wood craftsmanship

RELIGION: Neoclassical furniture

CAREER: Furniture maker; auction chairman

LITTLE-KNOWN FACT: Is a published author

TV SHOW: *Only Fools and Horses*

LIKES: Neoclassical furniture

DISLIKES: IKEA

TRAVEL: Dorset

INFLUENCES: Jesus, David Lynch

INFLUENCED: Ron Swanson

PRAISE: Said the one man who read Dave's book about furniture, "It was rather interesting, if not what I entirely expected."

David Armstrong-Jones, Viscount Linley

David Albert Charles Armstrong-Jones, Viscount Linley

Born 3 November 1961, Dave is the son of Princess Margaret, Countess of Snowdon and Antony Armstrong-Jones, 1st Earl of Snowden. He is the heir-apparent to the Earldom of Snowden.

An expert on chairs

Unlike other Royals, David found himself studying woodcraft in the small town of Beaminster in Dorset. With a passion for arts and craft, he would go on to design and make furniture before developing his own company, David Linley Furniture Ltd., known for its neoclassical designs and the use of inlaid wood.

Family

In 1993, David married The Honourable Serena Alleyne Stanhope. Together the couple have two children, Charles and Margarita. Hopefully, his marriage is a happier one than his ill-fated parents'.

If he was King

Barring some bizarre turn of events, this will never happen. But it would be good to see a king who could fashion his own throne. IKEA flat-pack rip-offs would sky-rocket, so even the common public could have their own imitation royal chair.

Charles Armstrong-Jones

The Honourable Charles Patrick Inigo Armstrong-Jones

Charles Patrick Inigo Armstrong-Jones was born 1 July 1999, the only son of Viscount and Viscountess Linley.

Royal matters

Like other royal children, Charles regularly attends events such as Trooping the Colour, a long and exhausting ceremony in which regiments of the British Army parade about marching in line, waving flags and doing things on horseback for apparently no particular reason otherwise than to celebrate Queeny's official birthday. Oh, and he has to spend Christmas in Sandringham with the family, most years too. Let's just hope Cousin Ed puts away the rifles before he gets stuck into the wine.

If he was King

Were he to take the throne today, King Charles Armstrong-Jones would be Buckingham's first prolific texter, so there'd be little time for official duties. The seventeen-year-old would probably be more concerned with updating his Twitter account, playing video games, and posting Snapchats of himself in compromising positions around the palace.

Fast Facts

FATHER: David Armstrong Jones, Viscount Linley

MOTHER: Selena Armstrong-Jones, Viscountess Linley

LINEAGE: Great-grandson of King George VI

SCHOOL: Eton College

HONOUR: Appointed First Page of Honour by Queen Elizabeth II

LITTLE KNOWN FACT: Inigo is a Greek name, and means 'fiery'. The name was given to Charles due to his father's love of 17th Century architect, Inigo Jones

LIKES: Video games

DISLIKES: Being told to switch off the video game console and come downstairs for dinner

FOOD: Pizza, McDonald's

SONG: *Teenage Dirt Bag*

MOVIE: *Die Hard*

BOOK: *The Catcher in the Rye*

RITE OF PASSAGE: Sitting through Trooping the Colour and Christmas with the Royals

DEFINING FEATURE: Being a sullen teen

Fast Facts

NICKNAME: Pizza pocket

FATHER: David Armstrong Jones, Viscount Linley

MOTHER: Selena Armstrong-Jones, Viscountess Linley

HONOURS: The day her father becomes the Earl of Snowdon, her title will change to Lady Margarita

LITTLE-KNOWN FACT: Named after Princess Margaret

CLAIM TO FAME: Being 'that poor kid' on the bike rack

LIKES: Her many middle names

DISLIKES: Her first name. It's a cocktail. And it doesn't sound very British, does it?

DEFINING FEATURE: Wavy blonde hair

MOST KNOWN FOR: Being a bridesmaid at the wedding of the century

FOOD: Boiled lollies

IF SHE COULD CHANGE ONE THING: She would like a bike of her own

HOBBIES: Picking flowers

MUSIC: Deep house

FAVOURITE COLOUR: Anything fluro

SOCIAL CONCERNS: Ensuring other children aren't forced to sit on the luggage rack of their fathers' bicycles

Margarita Armstrong-Jones

The Honourable Margarita Elizabeth Rose Alleyne Armstrong-Jones

Margarita Elizabeth Rose Alleyne Armstrong-Jones was born 14 May 2002. She is the second child of Viscount and Viscountess Linley. She is also the first of three granddaughters to the Earl of Snowden and the only granddaughter of Princess Margaret.

All in a name

Like many Royals, you need a few spare minutes to get through Marg's entire name. But behind each one lies a special meaning. Alleyne was chosen in honour of her mother, who shares the same middle name. Elizabeth is a nod to her great-grandmother. And Rose, according to her father, was handpicked by none other than her (at the time) three-year-old brother, Chuck.

Life so far

Margarita's life has already been filled with the kinds of events we expect from most royals. She's been embroiled in a tabloid scandal (a photo emerged of her seated on the luggage rack of her dad's bicycle, causing quite the stir), and she was a bridesmaid at the Duke and Duchess of Cambridge's wedding.

Margarita will turn 16 this year, so the Royals are holding their breath to see which side of the adolescent coin she will fall: well-behaved madam or rave anthem-mad socialite. Insiders are fearing, and the paparazzi are hoping for, the latter.

Lady Sarah Chatto
The Lady Sarah Frances Elizabeth Chatto

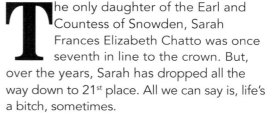

The only daughter of the Earl and Countess of Snowden, Sarah Frances Elizabeth Chatto was once seventh in line to the crown. But, over the years, Sarah has dropped all the way down to 21st place. All we can say is, life's a bitch, sometimes.

Sarah was a bridesmaid at Prince Charles' and Lady Di's wedding back in 1981. She met her husband, actor Daniel Chatto, while working on the set of the romantic epic film *Heat and Dust*, in 1983.

Fast Facts

FATHER: Antony Armstrong-Jones, 1st Earl of Snowdon

MOTHER: Princess Margaret, Countess of Snowdon

RELATIONSHIP: Daniel Chatto

CHILDREN: Samuel and Arthur Chatto

PROFESSION: Painter and Vice President of the Royal Ballet

LITTLE-KNOWN FACT: Despite receiving little media attention, Sarah keeps in close contact with Queen Elizabeth II

LIKES: Hanging out at the palace with Aunt Liz

DISLIKES: Dentists

Samuel Chatto

Samuel David Benedict Chatto is the son of not only an artist, but an actor as well. With that in mind, what can we really expect from the poor boy? Well, being a Royal, Sam will have plenty of opportunities to show us just what he's made of somewhere down the royal line. For now, though, the twenty-year-old is a little preoccupied with other matters. You know, like girls… and booze.

Fast Facts

DOB: 28 July 1996

NICKNAME: Sammie C

FATHER: Daniel Chatto

MOTHER: Lady Sarah Chatto

LINEAGE: Great Nephew of Queen Elizabeth II

EDUCATION: Westminster Cathedral Choir School; University of Edinburgh

RELIGION: Ministry of Sound

FOOD: Overcooked, deep-fried pub gristle

DRINK: Whatever's on tap at the student union bar

RELATIONSHIP: Netflix and chill

KNOWN FOR: Using his royal status to get likes on Tinder

Arthur Chatto

On the same day that Arthur Robert Nathanial Chatto was born, American boxer, Mike Tyson, was being sentenced to a year behind bars. Coincidence? An omen of sorts? Somehow we doubt young Arthur's life is going to be quite as dramatic as that of Iron Mike's. But, hey, he is a Royal after all.

But, no, no, we're just kidding. All evidence thus far points to the fact that, like his father and his father's father and every male member of the Royal Family really, Artie is developing a refined appreciation for a good, bland, monochrome jumper. And people who wear nice, boring clothes rarely ever go to prison.

Fast Facts

DOB: 5 February 1999

NICKNAME: Archie C or, when he's wearing a hat, Chat in the Hat

FATHER: Daniel Chatto

MOTHER: Lady Sarah Chatto

LINEAGE: Great Nephew of Queen Elizabeth II

EDUCATION: Westminster Cathedral Choir School

LIKES: The internet

DISLIKES: School photos

KNOWN FOR: Being a typical teenager: the reason there's now a lock on the liquor cabinet

Prince Richard, Duke of Gloucester
His Royal Highness The Duke of Gloucester

Richard Alexander Walter George was christened on 20 October 1944 at an undisclosed location. This was due to the fact that during the time of his birth a little skirmish known as World War II was playing out across the globe. Officials were a little hesitant to give out information concerning the Royals at that time. Pretty understandable, if you ask us.

In 1972, after the sudden death of his brother, Richard gave away his career as an architect to take on Royal duties and devote his life to the Crown. In 1974 he became Duke of Gloucester, Earl of Ulster, and Baron Culloden.

Fast Facts

FATHER: Prince Henry, Duke of Gloucester

MOTHER: Princess Alice, Duchess of Gloucester

LINEAGE: Grandson of King George V and Queen Mary

RELATIONSHIP: Brigitte van Deurs

CHILDREN: Alexander Wilson, Davina Lewis and Rose Gilman

EDUCATION: Wellesley House School; University of Cambridge

HOBBIES: Motor sports

TRAVEL: Lived in Australia for two years while his father was Governor-General

LITTLE KNOWN FACT: Published three books of photography

Major Alexander Windsor, Earl of Ulster

Alexander Patrick Gregers Richard Windsor is the heir-apparent to the dukedom of Gloucester. Of those Royals to have seen active military service, Al might be the realist of dealists. From 1998 to 2003, with the King's Royal Hussars, he experienced combat in Northern Ireland, Kosovo and Iraq, before retiring from the British army in 2008 leaving with the rank of acting major.

Fast Facts

DOB: 24 October 1974

FATHER: Prince Richard, Duke of Gloucester

MOTHER: Brigitte van Deurs

CHILDREN: Xan Windsor and Cosima Windsor

RELATIONSHIP: Claire Windsor, Countess of Ulster

EDUCATION: Eton College; King's College London; Royal Military Academy Sandhurst

HONOURS: General Service Medal; NATO Kosovo Medal; Iraq Medal; Queen's Golden Jubilee Medal; Queen's Diamond Jubilee Medal; Participation Award from Eton's year-end Swimming Carnival

SOCIAL CONCERNS: Director of Transnational Crisis Project

BEST KNOWN FOR: Sitting behind the Queen during her televised Diamond Jubilee service

Xan Windsor, Lord Culloden

So there's a Royal named 'Xan'. Will they ever cease to amaze? Some believe that Xan Richard Anders Windsor's first name is merely a shorter version of Alexander, in honour of his father – Major Alexander Windsor. However, at least one Buckingham source claims that the name is actually derived from the Olivia Newton-John musical spectacular, Xanadu, his father's favourite film.

Come on Major, tell us the truth, there's no need to hide this side of you. It's… metro.

Fast Facts

DOB: 12 March 2007

FATHER: Major Alexander Windsor, Earl of Ulster

MOTHER: Claire Windsor, Countess of Ulster

NICKNAME: X-bo

RITE OF PASSAGE: Xan is second in line to the Dukedom of Gloucester

MOVIE: *Grease*

LIKES: Roller skating

DISLIKES: Homework

IDOL: Captain America

RELATIONSHIP: Action figures

Lady Cosima Windsor

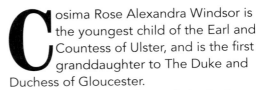

Cosima Rose Alexandra Windsor is the youngest child of the Earl and Countess of Ulster, and is the first granddaughter to The Duke and Duchess of Gloucester.

At only six years of age, little Cosie hasn't been all that articulate about what she wants to be when she grows up just yet. Currently she's still trying to figure out where Sesame Street's Count von Count fits in the Royal hierarchy.

Fast Facts

DOB: 2 May 2010

NICKNAME: Cosie Cosie Cosie! Oi! Oi! Oi!

FATHER: Major Alexander Windsor, Earl of Ulster

MOTHER: Claire Windsor, Countess of Ulster

POWER PLAY: Keeping it low-key and staying out of the press

EDUCATION: School of life

DRINK: Juice box

RELIGION: Sesame Street

CHARITABLE VENTURES: Sometimes helps Mum water the house plants

INFLUENCES: Little Miss Muffet

INFLUENCED: Yet to be seen

TRADEMARK: The curtsy

Lady Davina Lewis

Davina Elizabeth Alice Benedikte Lewis is the eldest daughter born to Prince Richard, Duke of Gloucester and Brigitte, Duchess of Gloucester. She is the sister of Major Alexander Windsor, Earl of Ulster.

In 2004, Davina married a Kiwi by the name of Gary Lewis. Together the pair have two children, Senna and Tāne. Gary's father, Larry, was the 1982 runner-up at The Golden Shears International Shearing and Woolhandling Championships. If you don't know what that is, don't worry, it's a New Zealand thing.

Fast Facts

DOB: 19 November 1977

FATHER: Prince Richard, Duke of Gloucester

MOTHER: Brigitte, Duchess of Gloucester

CHILDREN: Senna and Tāne Lewis

EDUCATION: Kensington Preparatory School; St. George's School; University of the West of England

LITTLE-KNOWN FACT: Davina's husband, Gary Christie Lewis, is a nephew of the New Zealand author Witi Ihimaera, one of the most prominent Maori writers alive today

ADDITIONAL FACTOID: By marrying Gary, Davina is the first member of the Royal Family to be married to someone of Maori ancestry

MOVIE: *The Lord of the Rings* trilogy

INTERESTS: Sheep shearing

Senna Lewis

The first child of Lady Davina and Gary Lewis, Senna Kowhai Lewis has spent the majority of her first five years being one of the more adorable youngsters present at Royal events. While, like her mother, it's unlikely she will ever grow up to represent the Crown in any official capacity, Senna will certainly be a most sought-after guest to attend all those soirees and luncheons.

And, why not? Have you seen this girl? She's gorgeous!

Fast Facts

DOB: 2 June 2010

FATHER: Some bloke from New Zealand named Gary

MOTHER: Lady Davina Lewis

LIKES: Finger painting

DISLIKES: Not having enough time to finger paint

TRAVEL: New Zealand, England

DEFINING FEATURE: Cuteness

TALENT: Being able to wear anything (including bucket hats) and making it look awesome

Tāne Lewis

Tāne Mahuta Lewis is the first son born to Dav and Gaz. He's linked to the Royals like all the rest, but this far down the list who can really tell who's who? We've stopped trying to figure it out, honestly.

What we can tell you, though, is that Tāne's name is in honour of Tāne Mahuta, the oldest living kauri tree in the world, which can be found in the Waipau Forest in New Zealand's North Island. The tree is estimated to be 2,500 years old.

Fast Facts

DOB: 25 May 2012

FATHER: A Kiwi called Gary

MOTHER: Lady Davina Lewis

NICKNAME: "Sorry, what's your name again?"

INTERESTING FACT: In Maori mythology, Tāne is the god of forests and birds. The tree which little Tāne is named after, Tāne Mahuta, translates to mean 'Lord of the Forest'

KNOWN FOR: Sometimes picks his nose and eats it

PASTIME: Teaching people how to correctly pronounce his name

LIKES: Tree-hugging

DISLIKES: Tree surgeons

FAVOURITE HEMISPHERES (RANKED): South, North

PARTY TRICK: Revealing his royal lineage to his mates

Published in 2016 by Smith Street Books
Melbourne | Australia
smithstreetbooks.com

ISBN: 978-1-925418-07-1

CIP data is available from the National Library of Australia.

Publisher: Paul McNally
Design concept: Hugh Ford
Design layout: Heather Menzies, Studio31 Graphics
Illustrator: Oslo Davis
Writers: Tobias Anthony & Jeremy Cassar
Senior Editor: Lucy Heaver, Tusk studio

Printed & bound in China by C&C Offset Printing Co., Ltd.

Book 8
10 9 8 7 6 5 4 3 2 1